Writing In The Dark

In a way, you could call it Rock Bottom.

Edited by Ian Crossland and Bill Ottman

Thanks to CreateSpace.com for allowing a place to self publish.

PREFORWARD

I had to write a second forward. A pre-forward or an after-forward. I wrote two books. Well, typed one based on the original. I tried to keep it as true to original as possible but there were some misspellings and odd things that needed touching up.

So it's an edit. An editorial on a story I told. It's basically the same book. Feel free to read the PDF scanned version of the original. It'll be available somewhere.

Well, I don't want to take up too much of your time. The other forward talks about how I feel, so I'll let you turn the page.

Special thanks to Carthage 521 on Myrtle for letting me hang out there.

FORWARD

I'd been advised to enter some sort of forward, and as I'd thought about doing it I went ahead and did it.

This book is a narrative poem. The kind of book you can open to any page and read any passage. Things were not made to make sense. There are also misspellings. They are intentional.

It details just under two weeks of life on the streets of New York City. A white kid with rich parents, pretending to struggle (though I don't actually think anyone's white). You see, as much as I want to understand the plight of the disenfranchised, the drug addicted and the psychotic, I am terrified to actually put myself on the street. To sleep alone at night, using my backpack as a pillow.

I've been lucky to have been given the things I've been given and I don't think throwing them all away will do me much good. Of course, there are two sides to a coin and this is a taste.

Life is Good

Just had a conversation with a great man. He is turning 5 on November 21.

Ackim was his name. His cousin is Ryan and his sister is Sarah.

They are really cool, adventurous and super heroes.

Today my car was stolen by the tow company. Unfortunately, I don't know my license plate number, and all reference points (DMV, tow yard) were closed and will be closed until after Labor Day. That's three days. Could be a rough weekend or could be a great weekend. I'm writing a book.

I just arrived at the Brooklyn Public House with Bill and Lauren. We're working on internet journalism. We're talking Kickstarters.

Looking through your apartment of ideas

-Sail (AWOL Nation) – Flying Squirrel video

I've exhausted myself thinking about Kickstarter ideas but it excites me that we could kick start apps.

We're walking back to Bill and Lauren's house, just arrived. Their roommates are Lauren and Ean. Strange world we live in.

Toxicity shuts us down to synchronization. In the form of food or energy.

Energy probably isn't "always" electrons. So, subatomic structures (quarks, gluons, fermions, etc.) would be energy structures too. Too hard to tell at this juncture.

We're always synchronized though. Awareness of it is what changes. Fluoride – toxic. A different material in water bottles. No more BPA

EST theatre is good. Ensemble Stage Theatre.

3

They're doing stories, now, about the matrix. The real matrix. You can access the internet through your glasses.

Are we really headed toward a society where people are controlled by what they control? By being so fixated on completing a task that the task becomes them?

I suppose we are to become what we want to become.

I need to find a place to stay. A drink of alcohol? I wonder if that's going to set me off or if the act of wondering, itself, is what does me in.

BAI

Make thumbtack speakers for laptops. Adapter for computers to transmit to speakers wirelessly.

Offer X

Offer 'X' amount of money reward to smash up
apartment

-Get Thomas Johannson a $6 million dollar jet and
fuel

I know any energy that comes at you is strange but
it's the energy around you.

Strange, the binds love it.

Would Edgar Allen Poe would be famous today.

We were very much insurgents when we defeated
the English Empire by winning the hearts of people.

Bleach is bad in the bloodstream because of the
ammonia the mind produces. Pre-frontal cortex and
Thalamus.

-Which direction is up? The direction above you or away from the earth's core?
-There is no up
-only Down

Membering increases the group. Remembering reduces the group.

It's weird not having my stuff. Weird censoring myself and not saying (illegible)

There's a difference in explaining that a person's behavior and a person are different.

Market cheap, marketable space pens

Good movie. A person dealing with a gravity pen.

Gravity's kind of like slavery.

Oc-ular-upy

Kickstarter – Pump water in to the ground

Spray water into the ionosphere and/or ozone

It's sunburnt right now, the earth.

If you read the temperature of the earth it would get hotter. But it's enervation – (while spraying water in the ozone).

Resting my spinal cord is important. Ocular activity strains the brain stem. (Sometimes) Sometimes focus (ocular) can bring better comfort so it goes both ways. Psychology.

Ocular & occupy. I write with the book straight up.

Occult

I love the occult. Why not the occolt. Oh the colt.
What a horse.

Any way. People are fucking animals.

Culture. Occupance. Creationism. The Color
Green. Love It.

Blue Green Occult. Blue River Oceans.

Oc Ocean Octane Octagon Ox

Old Oncology Ote Otter(man) Ottman. Oc is as the
ocean, Ot is the river.

Occult is the depths of the ocean.

It's better than the internet, this writing. At least I'm
not staring at a screen. Ah, the addictions of reality.

Comma

I really feel the pull of a comma. I don't care what I'm doing. I dig fast.

Ah, Ethan.

Eating. Word Association is fun

Less is more.

The first of the last.

The last word of a sentence is the first word of the next.

I like keeping my prourenent in the depths of reality.

It's like a weird ward being in a situation that has no blood. Where nothing is determined.

The date doesn't matter.

It's like impulses come and you have to decide
which to integrate width.

You have to be a good guy.

But you don't have to try.

You really decide which abilities, impulses you
attach to.

Assign to. Address to. Align. Assumption.

I am not using unnecessary space.

I am writing normal.

Write is "it" Wrist_Wring. Wren. Why? Wrye.
Whrychious. Hidious. Fixing & redoing this shit
makes it look like a math teacher. Ad dendum.

Ad Nauseum

I am homeless.
I am feeling fine <u>because</u>
- I have good cycle control
- I have very good addadum
- I am Alive
- It's never the same the second time
- I am alive
- I am a good person
- I am alive
- I am guitar
- I am gen
- uine
- ious
- epiphany I am alive
- I am good – it's excessive
- I owe you a page of goodness
- I owe you alive
- I am relaxed ing the muscle
- resting my eyes while liooking
- looking_lurking
- lurking
-
- Develop a thought that eavelops the thought
  process
  with clarity
  without complexity

Complexity

When people try to drive home a point, that is them
draining in a thought process.
Driving.
Drilling.
It's a game, this writing, like draining home a song.

Good posture -

The difference between breathing in your nose and
out your mouth

What percentage do you breathe out your nose?
Mouth?
20, 40?
2% 4%

Breathing out too much hydrogen can daze you
because it is so light weight. It doesn't weigh so
much and

your deep core is your methane production
laboratory

The weight of methane is 10x that of hydrogen.

So breathing

The philosophy. Light as air.

To go back and to go forward.
That's where we're at.
Because when you go forward it gets you where
you're going

As it moves away, it gets bigger; so it always seems
like it's in the same place - even though it's
traveling

It's ice. Cold.

Because isn't cooling down tadamescent to moving
away from

Moving away from is a reduction of heat so ... ...

13

Part of everything is moving away from you
because it is spinning

I'm in the lobby of Monica's place. I've decided to
write about What IS.

She is asleep. My car was towed for sure.
Standing.

No Standing any time means your car can't sit there.

Apparently you need a rocket scientist to figure this
shit out around here

It was a dance they were doing. A rythmatic
pulsation that created form.

Bleach is extremely good for you in small amounts.

It's very good

A hill is sadness if you see it like a frown.

Awareness is a level of DNA activation.
Or (de)activation

Compartmentalizing activity

I'm not sure what happens when you activate (all)
your DNA but I believe it gives you awareness of.

Someone that has activated and manicured their
DNA has a great sense of awareness, potentially

DNA activation is memory

Where the bottom hits the top

There's a chemical reaction on the surface of any situation, which is why it's different than below. Some may say it's just different, but there is a reason molecules hold together in to a surface structure.

If I knew, I'd write it here.

I think it has to do with quarks. And gluons. Maybe I just like those words.

I've also noticed how heavy asphalt is. It hangs right up over the road and smells

I realized last night, deep within the bowels is your methane production chamber. When you breathe it out your sense of smell improves.

In some sects of yoga, or body work out, they call it lotus position.

Working your deep core

It's one of those things where the lead-in is not that difficult but the move itself works out a muscle so hard.

Also, probably easier to do on an emptyish stomach.

One thing I like about writing on paper as opposed to typing on a computer is that when I make up words, like "emptyish," it doesn't underline them in red.

So I've made a point of this book to talk about what is.

Since this book is timeless, I'm allowed to go back through and write about anything I've written about before.

So I'm going to write about the matrix. A matrix.

To read the Matrix (A 3D matrix) you need 3 pieces of information. Where things are located. What it is composed of. And how much of it is there.

By knowing these things you can map how much Hydrogen, Oxygen, etc. is in a given spot, basically translating what is where.

To read the third dimension like a fourth dimensional being you need to center everything around you. As if everything was the center point.

Imagine

There is a conundrum in our 3rd dimension where we only see it from one perspective. Even when we see it from another perspective, we're still only seeing it from one perspective.

Imagining it from multiple perspectives at once is a step towards transcendence – or at least another perspective/dimension.

Funny how imagination is such an important tool but people ridicule things like imaginary friends. It's like people are afraid of the power of imagination because it is so much greater than them.

Uncontrollable, almost, like an inflating balloon.

I was thinking that ideas were like balloons. If you hold them too tightly, you pop them.

Balloons

If you let them go, they fly away.

If they fly too far away from the center, they explode.

Controlling an idea is a nasty task. It's a string membrane, floating around taking up space. Causing gravity. Vortextual.

Some people have deep thoughts, like whirlpools.

Maybe I should sell my car.

I'm faced with so many potentials right now, ranging from going to the woods, getting an apartment, staying with friends, sleeping in my car. Hijacking my parents' house while they're out of town, borrowing money.

Money

Is not a bitch.

Faith based currency is not killing me. But let's talk about what it is doing.

-Giving me confidence
-A sense of self worth.
-Right now I am worth $170.
-It will cost me $220 to get my car out of the tow yard.
So I am worth -$50

I prefer to be worth my pen.

But, then, if I lose that, what am I worth.

I suppose it's time to let go of self worth & survive.

But there is a worth, to synchronize with the world. Take from it and give to it.

It was relieving to find out my car was towed rather than stolen. I am integrated in a network of people and I love their pets & their trees. And their dirt.

People don't own that stuff beyond being guardians to it.

To master the matrix we must own it. Protect it.

Understand it and live it.
Manipulate it for the betterment of all. Not so much for some that others suffer, unless they are willing.

Give a little bit of yourself so that others gain much.

Part of being wealthy & powerful – describe it how you like – is that you can sacrifice a small amount to give certain people huge advantages

It takes work to acquire things and it takes work to let them go.

It's the best kind of work in my opinion. To see others' faces, or not.

To believe that what you've done has helped someone. To know it has.

Still, it's a theory. To maintain your own generation of wealth is important so you can keep giving.

If you stop taking from the earth, the earth no longer needs you.

I've noticed that in relationships, too. When you take, it gives the relationship credence. Too much thanks is unnecessary. Perhaps, thank by giving back.

One man's take is another's give.

So we are built to do.

23

Funny how that is the case.

A great learning experience, or relearning, was to find the balance in giving & taking.

I took too much, then I gave too much. It is time to take again but then giveness is divine.

If you take poison away from someone, are you not giving them life?

Maybe, or maybe it is their job to take the poison in small amounts until they become immune to it. That's what I like to do.

Though when toxic energy (over heatedness) is taken away from me, it is orgasmic.

The body literally rivets.

Shakes and pulses as the energy drains.

You can obviously drain yourself, take hot energy
out of your neck and in to your hand. Breathe it
out. Send it in to the ground or around you.

People are very good at draining your energy and it
is often good to let them.

We are storage capacitors. Batteries. Conductors
and superconductors. The energy flows within us,
through us and around us. Our storage capacity is
immense. We are capable of over charging despite
our defense mechanisms.

I think, sometimes, that over heating comes from
too much acid in the diet.

That chemical reaction is hot. Can be.

Toxic energy. Is it compacted? What makes it toxic? Amount? Consistency? Placement? Are they all different terms for the same thing? The way the energy is presented? Surely, energy itself is not toxic without context?

What's the difference between a statement and a question, and what happens when you put a period at the end of a question or a question mark at the end of a statement. I'd like to know more, beyond my intuition?

I prefer a statement. To a question.

A state to a quest.

My quest log is full. I (not really "full") need to answer some questions. Complete some quests.

The Holy Grail is filled with water. I solved that quest.

I'm on a quest right now to find out how to feel perfect.

Is the nature of feeling good to feel bad. Up, without down, would not exist. Binary nature.

Duality. Two perspectives make one. Maybe it's not redundant. As it seems.

Yes, there is more to you than just you.

Beyond being perfect, what can I do? By "perfect" I mean to hit all the marks I've set for myself. A subjective perfection.

Infect – A totally subject perfection.

I really love my brain stem.
I know there's levels of ammonia flowing through it.

Sometimes I forget how connected the body is.
Like when you have a sore neck, it's connected to
your lower back. You can work & work on your
neck, but unless you treat the source, the treatable
issue will return.

But, then, if I didn't have a sore spot to treat what
would I do with myself.

Tonight we check out performance art. Like
checking a book out of the library.

When I was really young, I was very right brained.
I knew what people were stressed out about and
would call it out. Even my parents didn't like it.

I learned at a very young age (2 or something) that left brained logical activity was super important for longevity.

"Out thinking" an opponent, so to speak.

I heavily over compensated and became very logical and concrete in my thought process.

Only recently have I re-engaged my right brain. I feel the energy flowing from left to right brain and vice-versa. The knowledge that comes without, through. Trust it because it's half of you.

On the Q train. My shirt says element. It's the only shirt I have. The others are in the tow yard.

Since I've been writing I've decided that my clothes are going to get inked up and I'm not going to worry about it.
Like a painter getting paint all over his shit.

(I drew some stuff in the original manuscript)

When I draw, I want to fill the negative space without drawing through what's already been drawn.

Like a long winded dream.

I have to remember my posture. I keep looking down to write when I sit and my neck cramps. No more cramps.

Monica's a healer too.

I enjoy laying hands on healing. On myself and others. Something about the differential in pH level (that's potential of hydrogen) makes it interesting when laying hands on others.

I like catching smells in the city that remind me of Venice beach. Maybe I'm just smelling myself.

I'm sure I've still got a bit of Venice beach in me. That shit sticks with you.

I notice, when I cross the Whitestone Bridge, driving in to NYC, I smell garbage. I think it's because there's a garbage dump there. I used to think it was the smell of the city.

Man, thinking and rethinking really causes tension.

Thinking about doing something, then not doing it, then thinking about it again. Not good for you. Maybe in small amounts it's good for you, like a fantasy.

Fantastic.

When I stretch my neck back I really feel like I am releasing some toxin out my lymph nodes that people don't necessarily smell, but that they register.

If we consciously, actively smelled everything around us all the time we'd probably go insane.

Desensitization is a survival mechanism. Like cutting down a tree to make room for a house.

Destruction. Deforestation.
Decriminalization

Sometimes I will sit so still for so long that everything will pass by. I would assume some things get caught in my filter but when there's a perfect breeze...

A perfect storm. And perfection is a subjective infraction. A nuisance. A troublesome bulwark. I like it. It gives me something to do.

I smell fungus when I clear my gut out. Which leads me to believe there is fungus in my gut. Spores of some sort. If they can survive in deep space they can survive in my gut.

I don't hate compacting energy. I like it, because it gives me something to release. The ticket is to remember to release it.

Subway performers. At least three part harmony, possibly four. These guys are rocking.

I like subway performers. These guys' harmonies are tight. They are a few feet away. Right in front of me. He's a rock in a weary land. That should happen more, but they have other trains to perform.

Other trains of thought.

I think, sometimes, about doing performance art on the train, but then I try to avoid annoying that one person out of 20.

I seem to like the release of energy so much that I constrict myself to prolong it. Something I change, because if you release it normally you'll get another chance to build it back up. No point in stressing the system for a jolly.

Good thing we have scanners. I don't feel like retyping this. Why would I, anyway, when I could produce the original.

I can put my Flip cam in my glasses case to avoid scratching the lens. I am not restricted to glasses in glasses case.

Tool is Loot spelled backwards. Also, toot is a palindrome.

I'm drawn to coffee. The smell.
Maybe it's the caffeine. Cafe.
It's a psychoactive drug. The only legal one, currently, in the United States (of America, I'm not sure about Mexico).

The debate, now, is to become a bartender

To live in the city and envelop the city life. Be enveloped by it.

It's probably my tendency to fight the forward
momentum. I've got to follow my heart path.
Make my memories my reality so my heart doesn't
have to work so hard.

Forward momentum can be dangerous if it doesn't
fit with your form. Being dragged in to situations.

There are a lot of arguments about it. Doing
something instead of nothing. Doing the right
thing. Doing the wrong thing.
Which brings me back to still mind. Things will
pass you by. They come and go, unattached. If you
don't need them, they don't need you. Sugar is
bitter and acerbic.

I like relaxing. My mind moves, so it's necessary.
Almost indulgent.

Micro-movements produce third dimensional
stillness. Take it easy

It's a jungle. Like stampeding elephants on wheels.
These cars. I've never spent much time in the
jungle, but cats will jump on your back if they want
to take you out.

In New York you can pull bottles out of 6 packs and
buy them individually. The price usually ranges
from $1.50 to $2.50

I just signed up to do some performance

Craziest open mic I've ever experienced. Guy shot
us with champagne and put a hole in the wall.

I think that's what Dada was like.

I got really stressed out during that performance. What was going through my mind was "I hope my clothes don't get stained with wine." And "I feel bad for the hole the guy put in the wall."

I am fully disenfranchised by the city. A bunch of people patting each other on the back for doing crappy work. The internet art is similar, but it's easy to find the good stuff and x out of the bad stuff.

And here I am making moral judgments on peoples' behavior.

I'm so annoyed that I got my car towed because it's going to cost me the money I have to get it out.

Which means I need to get a job in the city or borrow money.

I was totally planning on vacating this shit hole.

Internet income. That performance put me in a bad mood. Or perhaps I put myself in a bad mood.

But, then, that's like saying "A guy hit me, and because I didn't move out of the way I hit myself."

Remind me again why I don't go to live theatre.

Bad art, in general, is hard to sit through. At least it was free. I think the birds at the park are more interesting.

If they're trying to prove something they already have.

I think I grew out of the city, like a pair of pants.

People seem surprised and hopeful that I'll stay, but that would be someone else's life I'd be living.

Onward and upward. To the infinite inclusion. Afar and awander I am. A stone in the pond. A lily lag. Monster.

After the show, people stand around to socialize and all I want to do is get the fuck out of there.

Sorry Charlie.

You don't have to be a peasant to get by, you just need to make something -
      that resonates
      in a healthy way

I'm not sure if I've grown in to a healthier being and that's why I am uninterested in crappy performances.

Or if I'm overstepping my bounds. Probably,
because it's honest. I'm doing something right.

I've never truly been independent. Always relying
on someone else's structure. Funny, entangled
society we live in. I live in.

I can see, at least. I can hear and see and smell.

I'm happy to know I can breathe.

I wonder what kind of energy I'm putting out.

Monica really wants to help me get a job
bartending. So kind. I'm not sure I want to suck
the sick tit of this shit.

I could go cut some wheat and grind it into flour.
But I'd need to grow it, and that takes time.

I am a big fan of making my own entertainment. To a fault, maybe. To the point where I will fuck with people to see their reaction.

I fit in to modern American society in a really strange way. I'll stretch every day. While I'm out. Right now I am putting pressure on my neck to massage the lymph node. The adenoid? I love feeling my body in action.

If I had a tab for reality, I'd be buying drinks left and right.

It's easier to socialize when I'm drunk and easier to get drunk when I can afford it.

Maybe if I invest $20 of my wad in to drinks it will help me make some money, but, then, maybe that's alcoholism.

So many maybes. Maybies?

I feel so fucking limited, by myself! By myself.

Near myself. Along. Alone. A long lone. London.

I've noticed, when I lead with my left everything
starts to synch up.

Maybe from drumming.

I've thought of myself as right handed most of my
life and recently been getting involved in
ambidexterity. Abivilent dexterity, not quite, but
open to the change. It's like the world calls me.

Sometimes I pick up.

It's funny

It's funny how fire burns straight up. What is it?
Electrons? Dissembled carbon, or whatever's
producing the flame. It's reddish, yellow, blue,
white, red. Like the american flag. Stars and
stripes look like a burning fire.

Any way, it burns away from the center. Not
necessarily "lighter than air," though it may be. It
burns away from the center of the suck. Sucked
"up" (Away from) like anti gravity.

What is it escaping from? Pressure? I have a
feeling if you created a system, a pressurized
system, where there is a pressurized fire and a low
pressure side, it may burn sideways – though it may
still burn away from the earth's core. Too many
assumptions.

Without experimentation.

I guess there is a natural acceleration to a spiral,
which is why it expands or gets bigger.

I love how universes change and shift so abruptly.

Not sure if it's dimensional shifting. It must be
focal shifting. Maybe decision making takes
energy out of the surrounding area.

Oh, alcohol, you have done me.

I'm getting beer at the bar.
My plan is to throw caution to the wind, spend my
money and get a job.

I want to get paid for being. (Strong)
> -work out
> -manual labor
> -yoga
> -I guess it takes a consistent work force

Get that one hit song on the radio and retire. To what? Making another song.

I am writing a story about writing a song. Maybe cut out the story or maybe that is the song.

I can bury a lot. I love hearing people talk. I can tell that part of what they say is about me.

Market internet/networked white boards.

Monogamy is great

So I guess

Polygamy is great. Not.

Is great.

About to rock and roll.
Two Guinesses will do that to you.

The Guiness.

Guinea Pig. Papau New Guinea.

What's up with neck pain. When you turn your
head and it hurts real bad and it's warm and wet. It
can't be a good thing. What the fuck is it?

We're not Bears. Bears have great necks. A bear's
penis, apparently, has "guard hairs" that will rip you
apart if it fucks you.

I ordered a Wonton – Egg Drop soup. It's salty, but
good. There's beef in it. I think it's beef.

I get these quarts of Won-ton Egg drop soup and eat them. I love them. For $3.25 you can't go wrong.

Except making them yourself. Except you need the equipment. Deep fryer? Friar?

I've sinned, Friar. I've fried.

Friend.

Day 3 – Memorial Day

Monica has been a great host.
Her roommate gets back in to town tonight so I will be finding another place to stay.

Gotta find $50. To get my car outta hock.

We are going to check out the Labor Day Parade on Eastern Parkway. I hear it's like Mardi Gras.

It's a wet day. Must have rained earlier.

Look Ahead. Your wants and needs are very simple.

Great day at work. Love the bars in the area.

In a way, going in to bars and talking to people about getting jobs is the most fun.

A 3 dimensional slope is a helix.

Up or down
DNA Baby,

Hookah FTW

I'm sleeping in Bill's car.
Someone just jacked it from behind and woke me up. It's 1:18 AM. They were like "woah, I did NOT see that." I think they rammed his trailer hook up. Probably fucked up their front bumper if anything.

The cover of this notebook came off today. Apparently Bill and Lauren have a really attractive single roommate, yet I still sleep in the car. Her name is Camille.

My brain has been flushing out chemicals. I went and applied at many bars. Had a lot of drinks.

Had my first (or second) "Pickleback." Whiskey shot followed by a shot of pickle juice. Dill? Delicious.

Dill
One of my favorite weeds.

I felt like a football player today, trying out for the draft. Draft beer.

Monica came with me, showed me a bunch of bars in the area, from Washington to 4th Ave. Very promising.

I slept from (sleptember) 10:30 to when that guy hit the car. Had some nice dreams.

It's raining outside. I'm fortunate to have a dry place to sleep. Rock bottom would be sleeping on wet rock.

My parents offered to pay to get my car out of the tow yard. I owe them. They have treated me excellent.
Given me when I have not deserved it.

I have to treat the rest of society as good as they have treated me.

The lights are yellow, red and green. Street lights and traffic lights. White head lights. I gotta remember, it's not a stop light if it's green.

When I write, and tense up my hand, the center of my palm gets hot.

It's good to shoot energy out of it.

The city streets sound like an orchestra. There's enough light out here to write, where as in a dark room I may be blinded.

Oops

I'm looking forward to getting my laptop back. My whole car package. I've been wearing this Element t-shirt for days. The same Lucky Brand boxer shorts, the elastic is so stretched out.

I learned, when I sit on the toilet, if I let my legs fall apart it stretches the underwear elastic. Broken and severed many an underwear like that.

God Bless scanners.

A wet windshield kind of looks like the Matrix. A bunch of lines streaming down in synchratic order.

If Joe Pantiaglo, I think that's his name, were here, he'd say "With a green light shining through those water droplets it would look even more like the Matrix." (*editor's note – His last name is Pantoliano)

The light behind me keeps shifting from green to red, but it's not enough to bleed out the yellow street light in front of me.

The dripping water looks like people walking.

Sometimes, when I let my mind associate, I come up with some great stuff that didn't seem so great while it was incubating.

1-2-3

Sometimes, three unrelated thoughts form one great thought.

I smell mold on the blanket that used to barrier Bill and Lauren's room. I like using the word "barrier" as a verb. Was I supposed to say barricade?

Denim and leather, they both stretch.

But what are the threads of leather made out of? Skin cells?

I met a great bartender at the 4th Avenue Pub named Miranda, I think. She is a tattoo artist. Lives with three roommates in Bushwick.

I may move there, Bushwick.

Probably not in to her house, but, then, I'm not writing about what I'm not doing.

Jealousy must go.

Heads must be turned.
Jaws must be dropped.
Rings must be wrung and sows must be sewn.

Sews also must be sewn.

Wordiness is not my hefty strong suit, but that
hookah smoke is still in my system.

I love relativity. Shadows of raindrops look like
leopard prints on this page through the window.

I like how a dark letter shows up against a light
letter.

Don't push too hard, because if you make a mistake
you're going to have to push relatively harder to
make it better.

Don't screw yourself.

Or do. I'm trying to stay positive.

My resume's looking good these days. Putting Abigail on it was a great idea. We moved the open Mic to The Branded Saloon. Great Bloody Marys. $8. Not complaining.

I am, however, lauding them for their awesome Bloody Marys.

They'd hosted their softball team for a party. They came in 2nd this year. When I tried to find out who came in first, the guy didn't know.

I read some of this at the performance art piece (exhibit) last night. Just popped up and started talking about Nitrogen or Something.

I'm aware I hadn't written about Nitrogen before now. Maybe I've destined myself to read about it.

Let's talk destiny.

Destination.

Uber Nation.

I use these weird spacings.

Part of me is like "oooh yeah, I'm really flying through the pages now." The other part of me knows I'll be sad when the book's over.

The other part of me will keep writing.

I think of Sacred Fools in Los Angeles. Charles
Bukowski. Bukowsical. They did that. He drank a
lot of Alcohol and wrote. I guess I fit in with that
on some level.

Writing is like throwing a bucket of water against
the wall and watching it drip down. All the words
are different streams. Paths. There are so many.

Which one do you write? All of them I suppose.

I really love her, Rebecca Larsen. I hurt her pretty
bad. Sent myself in to a tail spin of what love is.

It's weird seeing your tail fly in front of you
because you're spinning so fast.

It's even weirder when your tail is big and bushy.

I'm trying not to put my toe print on the wind shield. I AM, however, trying to get comfortable.

There's nothing wrong with trying, by the way.

Yoda may have told you differently, but he was a 700 year old puppet.

An illuminati puppet. Speaking their wishes.

I'm going to spend some of my 30mb this month to download Roger if it's available.

Sometimes, when I smell card board, I think of pizza. I actually smell pizza. I associate it to all the pizzas I've ordered. In all the card board.

I leave a lot of room around the edges.

Sleepy time calls me. I answer and I'm like "hello?" They are like "What's up?" I am like "not much."

I've really gotta start writing apostrophes as apostrophes when there is an "S" at the end of a word and not use the S as the apostrophe. You could consider it a contraction, I suppose. In some future culture, it is.

The sun is like a street light. It's bright. I wonder how easy it is for flys to delineate. What a great word, by the way.

If Bill and Lauren ever need a place to stay, they can stay with me. Max would be proud. He probably is.

Pride is an issue. It's one of the Christian deadly
sins but an American past-time.

National Pride.

Take Pride in your work, you gluttonous fool.

Gluton. If that's not a word it needs to be.

I like light refraction. Dissension. Diffraction.
Refraction.

Part of writing in the dark means that the shadows
all look the same.

And yes, by "the same" I mean "similar."

Quotation Marks are unnecessary sometimes but I
use them anyway.

Like Christmas tree ornaments.

I put them on the tree. Host them like a web server.
Adorn them with lights and try them on like a beach
volleyball outfit in the gray sun and wet sand.

The sand's actually red(ish). It's nice and wet and
yellow and red. It flows through me like a lion's
mane. Loin's?

The real juncture is Tri.
There's two ways to choose, but there's the way you
came from. Ah, dissemination, at it again.

Sometimes, you let the thoughts drip away down
the back of your throat. I wonder what that muscle
is, right there, by the brain stem.

Mu

Muscle. Mucus.

Murder.

She'd be proud.

Mull it over. Don't worry about a thing.

But DO mail out what needs to be mailed.

Three things:

I like when things get real dark as my eyes focus. I like the floaty thing in your eye, and I like that wet, warm feeling you get in your neck when you turn your head too fast. Or too hard, or wrong or something. It hasn't happened to me in a while. I've been extra precaution.

Precaution and precognition.

I'm really heating up now.

I can smell the cardboard like it's baking.

I guess timelessness is the key. Write a book when you're ready, but prepare for ridicule from those that are stuck.

Some people get stuck in the mud and get pissed. Others work their way out. If you fall in quick sand, don't struggle. Relax. It's all you've got.

Use a stick and float on it. Always carry a stick when hiking. A nice wooden rod with all the accoutrement. Love the French.

Pardon Mine.

65

I'm not too worried about running out of space.

Time for a cool down.

Tesla – A man without time.

Lucky me. I stepped outside to cool down and noticed my hat had fallen on the ground. It was damp and cold from the rain. Now it's on my head and the world is new again.

A gain is an addition.

Sometimes it's best not to question "Why?" too much and just accept that it is.

You probably put it there to find it anyway.
Perspectively Inspective.

Speculate, Spect acular.

Where as it was blood boiling hot a moment ago, it is now ruminescant with the wet hat. I only wish it was dripping down my neck.

I'm going to take advantage of the rain. One of these days I'm going to write words in no particular order.

Let the letters hit the page like electrons in the double slit experiment.

Bombardment? Maybe it's refraction

(Yet again)

The shadow of water flies across the page like a shooting star of darkness. Looks so bright against the light.

Maybe it's not too late to get some electrolytes.

Brooklyn at night.

I'm not afraid. I am alight. And slightly afraid. I hear the roads are like jungles and the police are very kind. Like park rangers, always circling around.

It's like the last step before I jump becomes a paragraph of words.

Maybe I'm procrastinating the big one. I wouldn't put it past myself.

Alright. I'm at least going to get wet.

The mechanically separated chicken wasn't so bad. Vienna beef, they called it.

I feel poisoned. Not in a painful way, but in a way where it's difficult to finish words or phrases.

That is what some of society's food will do to you, I suppose. Slow you down. Make you miss a step. I wonder if they realize that's what Nitrates do. I wonder if that is what nitrates do.

The walk was invigorating and the beef was cheap. I also second guess. Was the door locked? Of course it is. I also purchased the strawberry banana juice. No complaints here. I was happy to upgrade to the Large for $4.

Here I am with the whole "eating meat" thing. I love meat. I don't like the the way animals are abused and turned in to food. I like stem cell meat growth.

Here is a quest I'm on. To go on a hunger strike. To actively stop eating meat until society actively begins.

To eat stem cell meat rather than pen up and eat animals. Cows. Chickens. Pigs.

People own them and want to keep owning them and selling them. I'm glad no one owns me.

Meat.

I have a feeling completing this quest would be worth an immense amount of experience. I don't know if I'm going to complete it though. It might be more trouble than it's worth.

We can expend our lives speeding up aspects of our evolution. Is it worth it? That's up to you. People are dynamic that way.

The tow truck just pulled up. Flashed some lights. Backed up and took off.

I thought the fellow behind me was going to get towed for a moment.
A minute, but not quite.
A minute minute. That's my newt.

Bill and Lauren's new roommate has a bird. I may have already gone over this, but I love her.

So what aspect of reality will you expend your life advancing? The arts? Which kind? I like to think of myself as a turtle. I watched that bird hop around and stretch out. I guess focusing on my own thing yields the most reward.

Earlier, to Bill, I seemed hyperactive. And I was. A lot of Nitrogen from the alcohol. A lot of thoughts outside myself. Stressing myself. I'm better off relaxing anyway. I have a lot of catching up to do. I owe society a great deal.

I spent a lot of time mooching. Thomas is right about that, there is no denying. I tricked myself in to believing (I prefer "in to" rather than "into" sometimes) that I was owed a restful existence because of all the YouTube videos I made. A selfish ordeal. To give is to get. We are not owed more than the skin on our back. And even then.

To contribute to society is important. And that usually means more than spending time with friends.

It would be nice if that were my job, but if it were wouldn't that take the fun out of it?

I am a pansy, that I don't like being forced to do stuff. A mild resistance that is far too long. Cumbersome, that's for sure. Let yourself be forced from time to time, I'm sure you will enjoy it.

I like meeting new people. Of course, they're only
new to me. To them they are old hat.

I don't mind frayed edges. They worry me if I have
an image to uphold. I don't like to hand a resume
with frayed edges, for example. Also, I don't want
the page to rip. Structural integrity is important to
me in that regard. I like the way they look though.
Frayed edges.

I wonder if Shannon will continue to Play
Stronghold Kingdoms. Obviously, the answer is
yes. Perhaps I've connected to him through the
verse. Maybe he is wondering where I am.

On the road. Standing is allowed here. I knew I'd
be on the road some day.

The temperature drops and I'm ok. For now.
Relativity sucks energy.

I remember when I learned that things didn't get colder. Only less hot. "Cold" isn't a thing. Only heat. Heat goes away or to. Good old electrons.

Someone's got to derive all the differences of what energy is.

It's the electron and the transfer of the electron. It's like the heat doesn't exist unless it's moving. Like motion, itself, is heat. Which is a kind of energy.

What, then, is potential energy? Stored heat? Stored where? And how is it heat if it's not moving? And if it is moving, it's kinetic. So energy is both possibility and actuality.

It sounds kind of vague to me.

The rain sounds like prickly fingers on my scalp.
Special thanks to Amanda for making me so artsy.
Being forced isn't so bad sometimes. Cut with the
grain. Turn and turn. Tourne.

That thought heated me up. Memories can heal you
and kill you. Regulate your temperature. Try.
Breathe out your mouth. Not only is Carbon
Dioxide heavy, but it's hot, due to the added
electron from oxidation. Lay it all out because
there's more to come.

Easy breezy. Life's too easy. I complicate myself
for fun and have learned so much from it. 2+2 is
still (1+1)2.

Since I was young I thought bananas tasted like
penicillin. Now I know why. Not exactly why, but
they are like an antibiotic. Get those ripe bananas.
They really taste like penicillin.

Or amoxicillin, which is some synthetic Penicillin.

Staring in to the unknown doesn't do too much good. Wondering what tomorrow brings causes a rush of adrenaline and makes me nauseous. It's easier to face the unknown when it's right in front of you.

Tomorrow is right here, in the shape of a car and a bundle of other things.

Don't get too hung up on the present, because that will change too.

I'm not here to tell you what not to do.

I've created a margin by folding the book in half. Something is always lost in the fold. Bless you.

I went through a phase where I stopped saying
"bless you" when someone would sneeze. I
thought it was a weird, trained behavior people had,
and did, without knowing what they were doing.
Then I thought it hearkened back to the plague. A
sneeze might mean your death in a time of great
sickness. Then I found out what a blessing really
was. Now I have no problem blessing people.

There's more to it than just saying it though.
There's an energy behind it. Lost in the fold.

People are arriving out of the fold. Everything is.
Everything is curved (to us) and is arriving and
leaving at the same (similar) rate. Quarks are
spinning. Everything is spinning to what we
perceive as a stand still. It's very placid when you
think about it.

Numerics kind of calm me. Like wind. Wound around the earth and through my hair.

Blowing wind and winding a toy. Wound so tight and wounded for evermore.

Just a bunch of words that are spelled the same. Similar. Simile.

Different tensions. Maybe our language is tensive.

Sometimes I punch myself in the nose without intention. I smell a ringing.

I guess when you're working hard, time stands still. But, then, it never does. Does it?

Moving to stand still. There's that ever present micro rhythm again. Not worried. Accepted. Accelerated.

Acuity and Acupuncture might do me a world of good. So says Monica. In my shoulder. Or I can stop pretending. Get back to basics.

My life ain't so bad. I figured out how to relax and so I will.

Releasing energy sure heats up the area around me. Which heats me up. That's using electrical heat and converting it to thermal heat. Something to do with water, stasis, static, vibration and hydrogen (obviously). Brings me back to pH (potential of hydrogen) and level of acidity. I'm going to master thermal conduction.

Internal gravity. A self sustaining ecosystem is your body. You receive energy from an external source, which causes your heart to beat and memories to form. Like your brain. It's a memory turned reality.

This energy and momentum causes blood to flow which causes convection.

It's easy to boil water, but not when it's flowing.

Count yourself lucky and keep your circulation going.

I must depart from this timeless reality for a moment.

Special Thanks to John's Doughnut shop on Myrtle for letting me use their bathroom.

Gotta love soap.

They also serve Greek Food. Looks like a great diner. I got a bagel, toasted, with cream cheese. It was $1.50.

I've burned through almost half the ink in this pen, assuming it was full when I started.

I'm sitting here at Fish & Sip in Park Slope. Two jobs on the horizon, one at Eve's Lounge and one at The Cherry Tree. Both bartenders.

I'll need access to my car. My clothes, particularly.

I went to the tow yard earlier and was told that I need to renew my registration in order to get it out. Or I could tow it out and pull the plates off.

I'm going to get a New York license while I'm at it. I borrowed massive money from my parents. I'm not happy about it and neither are they.

I'm inking up my clothes like a real artist.

The nice thing about writing instead of typing is that I don't have to save my progress.

That "Somebody that I used to know" song is really good. Reminds me of some Steely Dan shit.

Cigarettes, Newports, were $11.50 today. September 4, 2012.

I'm taking this Food Protection Course for bartending. Apparently, someone with a license needs to be on premises the whole time.

You are forced to spend 15 minutes or so on each page. I read it, took the quiz and got one wrong and must spend another 15 minutes. I disagree. I think I got the question right.

Food trucks don't need permits, but they're still food establishments.

I feel the clock ticking. Jobs don't start never. I will double negative you all night.

I really want to go to the subway under Times
Square and play some music. Gotta check these
voicemails.

Chilling at The Cherry Tree where I just got a job.
6-8 tomorrow. Love this town after a beer.

Tomorrow I focus on right now. I get my car, play
some tunes. There's an open mic tonight here. I
had my guitar on me so I'm going to play.

Quite a day, I spent on the internet working towards
getting my Food Protector's License. What a beast
that is. Gotta know pork's gotta be cooked at 155°F
for 15 seconds. Down with Trichinosis.

I'm really interested in this guitar on the street
thing. $3 in 25 minutes. Just about minimum
wage.

It's like a real life kickstarter. Attrition at its finest.

This place doesn't pay a shift pay but at least it's awesome. And the stadium's opening up next month. So rock.

It is a large venue. I'm changing pens. I don't have a point to prove.

When all else fails, write!
Even though nothing has all else failed.

Writing by candle light. It's fun. It's bright and it's dark all at interchanging intervals. Like a beast!

I'm deliriously writing. Three hours sleep. I could do this a lot. Maybe it's the beer.

I've been wearing this hat. I feel like that turtle that walks around in that hat. He sticks his neck out. His Adam's apple.

I think he puts his hands in his pockets, too. And slinks.

Maybe he wears a tie, too. I got a feeling I'm making that up, but maybe not.

I really like candles. Fire, in general. It's hot. It's bright. It's warm. It's light. It's Jesus's ghost on a silver platter. It's sliver. I like how it dances around, electromagnetically, but still affected by the wind.

Is that what fire is? Bridging the gap between convection and electrocution? Yeah. No. It's both.

How many times in a row can I contradict myself. The answer – I can't. LOLN – I have avoided making little sense to this point.

I am ready to party. On a microphone.

I will sing and scream and yell so loud.

I'm still perfecting that microphone singing. Gotta
Back off. And still play to the room. When I hit
the arenas I'll be able to back off and blow out.
Who's going to hear me? 20, 30 people. .001% of
the crowd. In a small room, if I blow out, everyone
hears it.

I'll do the half song twice in between the other two.

Getting ready. Let the adrenals flow!

The Brooklyn DMV is Awesome. They are good
people, and the system is fluid. Closes at 4pm.
Very communicative. They're always letting you
know what's up through the speaker and they are
nothing but helpful when spoken face to face.

I think the pen has gotten faded. It could be the damp paper.

I wonder if, after they close the doors at 4pm, anyone just can't take it and has to leave to use the bathroom. They will not be permitted back! Let them know.

This is a very intricate society. With all the payments, verifications, subsidies. Woven in like patchwork. All the dues and bills. Copies of this and that. Proofs of whatever.

Spending a lot of time at the Brooklyn Navy Tow Yard today. It'll be nice to get my car back. It will be nice to sit down somewhere that I own.

Life is much about variety. Too much sitting and I want to stand.

Too much white and I need black.

It's interesting to hear other peoples' stories. They get frustrated or they don't.

I'm going to eat peanuts tonight, I think. They're waiting for me in my car. I've been eating them with the shells, as per Bill's suggestion. They're good, fibrous and salty.

They've been cutting the plates off my car. If they'd asked, I would have taken them off for them.

I wonder what kind of tools they're using to cut my plates off. I have become a tow expert. I know the ins and outs of it.

The air's warm and wet, but I don't think it's going to rain just yet.

I guess it's humid because we're right near the water in this Navy Tow Yard.

I just got bit by a special black mosquito. It itches like hell but I'm not going to scratch it. Winner.

Living on the street is very different than living in a car. (It feels great to have a pen in my hand.) I realized this last night around 11 when a guy named Robert came knocking on my window in the rain. He was HIV positive and hadn't eaten since 10am. I know the pain. Fatigue sets in pretty fast if you only have crappy food once in a while. He said he was going to ride the train all night and make it look like his book had put him to sleep. He said someone told him I was laying in my car and looked like something was wrong.

After he asked for money I thought he was lying. I wonder.

By staying with friends and getting money from my parents, I have kept my spirits up. Slept on Monica's futon the last two nights. Car sleep for many nights before that. It's not bad, except a little cramped. I'm not complaining, just stating.

Did some landscaping up in Wilton for $100 at an organic grocery store. I really enjoy weeding. People keep urging me to speed up and pay me hourly but I insist to get paid for the job and take my time to get the weeds up. Get the roots. I like the feeling, and I don't like doing shoddy work.

I've been urged to eat Steak by Monica so I got a beef burger on DeKalb at Mike's Diner on the corner of Hall st.

I'm about to head down in to the subway to play so I kind of feel like I'm procrastinating. Since I got my car back I hadn't been writing as much. The burning urge is still there, though, and it really does feel good to hold a pen in my hand. Cramps aside, I'm building up my fireball shooting palm skill.

Bill is arrived home. I will change there and depart. Descend. Delight! DeKalb.

I guess, because of the unknowns, we are prone to forget certain things. We must choose what to forget. It is an election of the mind.

My shoes literally smell like fecal matter. I shit out my feet.

The idea is, when you decipher the matrix there are no unknowns.

You could think it was Just a girl

She was a girl what came in to my life. She was
just a gurl. Such a girl. I was in awe of her. She
seduced me. Like a wry hen. That girl. I could.

I'm eating peanuts, and apple. It is delicious. I'm
tasting what I ate earlier, it is that good. I love her.
I would do many things for her for myself.

Life is but a dream, a fabled portal of idiots. It is a
tale to be told of idiots. It is a Journal. You must
make more space. Enliven yourself. In this
Journal. Entry.

Taking a chunk of peanut then a bite of apple tastes
like pan cakes –.

You can write any way. Depending on how it looks it is more pleasing to watch.

It may not make as much sense but is easier to see.

Seeing is peeing ← Deflated Pee

Peeing is believing

Peeing is sensing

Organs inside you.

It's what you see. I will explain.

Seeing is a live reverberating (vibrating) off your eye. If you turn the frequency down it starts to vibrate and tingle your ear drums and you hear it.

Sometimes, to meditate, you exert the moment.

Which would mean outside in. Inheurting The moment

It was inspired by a lot of people.

Dang my shoes smell like shit. I gotta wrap them up, there's no baking soda.

So when you eat the peanut with the shell, you create a kind of butter with the oil. Salt helps get chlorine out of your system.

Apple and peanut tastes like so many things. The 6th dimension. What for it to smell like...

It tastes like coconut if you chew it enough. Every once in a while to let a big one through. Do you want to be a big one?

I think the shit in my shoes was taking a shit before.
Nasty shit. I washed my feet off earlier. I shook
some peoples' hands and the socks were two days
old.

It's more if you chew it oily it feels like coconut
when you swallow it.

Ok, late night wasted writing is a real roll of the
die. I'm on the PATH train, heading to Manhattan
from Jersey. I hurried on to the World Trade Center
bound train. I think it will be fine.

This last week has been interesting. I've been
eating too much refined sugar, spending too much
money. Maybe, because of the sugar, my willpower
is low. Maybe I just want to sleep for days. I hope
I don't freak people out that walk by and see me
sleeping in my car.

I don't want to start a panic.

If there's an easy way to the G train from WTC I am in luck. I hurried on to this train and realized the 33rd street one might have been better.

Waves of passion, waves of pregnance won't stay if you stand still.

Some of this stuff would sound great to music. I need to write a new song in the sunlight. Endorphins? It's such a generic term to describe so much more that's going on. I'm getting good at writing while walking.

Basically, don't stop to enjoy the music. Keep walking and take it with you. The benefit of making your own.

I'm going to apply for food stamps. I hadn't done it before because I felt like it kept me from making more than $1000 a month. Now, I plan on getting a job but using the food stamp money in the mean time.

What do you think about doing work you morally object to for money? Obviously, by the nature of the question, it is morally objectionable. I was looking for work at a vegan restaurant. Give those cows a break. I still am. I could cook at a restaurant. It's not as much money as the tips but it might be fun. I know enough about front of house that it would probably help expedite.

The coffee is making me feel high. Loopy. Caffeine, as it stands, is the only legal psychoactive drug in the United States of America. I apologize for the redundancy. I aim for concision.

I really don't know what's next. I've changed pens.
I smell my own body odor. I smell a familiar
perfume or lotion.

I think it is to find a sense of calm and/or peace. It's
Sept. 11, 2012 and we are going to check out the
memorial.

I've met some people that sleep on the train or in
the park. One woman asked me if I wanted a sex
massage. She was robbed while sleeping on the
train. It's a taste of what could happen if one were
to sleep in public with their things. More
dangerous than the jungle in a way.

I don't feel like wielding a phone call right now so I
turned my phone off. I'm lucky to have a phone.

Wealth gets passed from parents to children
sometimes.

An unsaid intricacy of our society.

At least with $4 you can buy a pen and a notebook and write a book.

The ability to produce. It's interesting. To take an, otherwise, blank slate and turn it in to something worth deciphering. It's a great thing to give to society. If not one's self.

I made a few videos but didn't upload them to YouTube (or any other site). I feel like it's self ingratiating. Also, I felt shame. I felt like I'm doing it to induce pity when my real intention is to share my experience.

I also feel like I'm expressing my laziness. I had an apartment from July 15 to Sept. 1.

I got a job that I knew would be easy and didn't get paid much for it, rather than do the hard work of applying to 20 busy restaurants, booking one and serving my ass off.

I could do it. The thought of riding the train 40 minutes a day is exhausting. Maybe it's not what I should be doing if I fear it this much.

But, then, maybe it is. Getting a job serving, wherever, commuting. Making bank. Getting a place. Making dinner. Having friends over. Spending time with them. Running camera for Minds. Buying my own camera. Setting up a studio in my apartment. Buying a house. Setting up shop and stability. The illusion of.

Ride the illusion.

Ride it

The illusion of stability has gotten me this far. Not
sure why it hasn't gotten me further. Why it would
or wouldn't.

Heated palms sweat. Choke up on the pen. Relax
the grip. Don't bruise the bones. Once they hit FA
209 something my food stamp interview is close.
I'll buy apples, and continue to give them away.

In a society where profit is requested you might not
find thousands of apple trees in central park. And if
you did, the apples will probably be picked and
peddled at the base of the tree. Like a factory shop.
At least the trees produce oxygen. God bless
America.

I would live in a tree. I had a dream last night
where my brother rebuilt our second childhood tree
house.

He built it much higher, in a different tree.

The truth is, the first one – the real ones – were not built in trees. They were built with wood. Does that make them tree houses?

I don't mind sitting around. It's nice to have something to do while doing so. I learned, while acting on television, – and theatre – a lot of your job is sitting around and being quiet. Even auditions. Socializing is important but missing your cue is basically a resignation letter.

Missing your cue by a few seconds in theater can be excessively entertaining but doing it on purpose is malicious. Not delicious.

Every once in a while I feel gravity tugging and twisting in my lower back. It really gets in there.

I got redirected to apply for public assistance. It offers $200 a month in rent plus food stamps and medicare. For living in a capitalist society, we have good social welfare. Welcare. Well fair. They will yell my name.

I remember being a kid. When my mom would yell for getting out of line. It's like nails on a chalk board when I hear a woman yelling at a kid like that. Part of why I'm not married. I don't want to be treated like that again.

I got afraid of cleaning out my ear with a q-tip (cotton swab) with people walking around me because I don't want someone to jack me on the side of the head and shove it in. Same reason I don't want someone behind me while I'm standing at great heights. An intelligent distrust? I've had people jokingly shove me before.

I saw a friend of mine while playing in the subway yesterday. Harry. We worked together at Porthouse – Summer theatre in Ohio. He pulled out his instrument to play. It was great.

I think I figured out, with an acoustic guitar, the best place to play for tips down there is on the platform where the trains come. I experimented. Played there, upstairs in the common area, (too loud there and everyone's busting ass to get somewhere) and up on the surface. Side of the road on 7th Ave. and at Times Square. Just be sure to stay on the sidewalk next to a legitimate roadway. All my friends have day jobs. That is not true, but one of them does.

When you look at someone it gives them a stage.

Remember, don't pay attention to someone that is acting out because it will give them a reason to keep doing it. Seeking approval. I try to play with the same fervor whether there is someone watching or not. Making eye contact, though, it can cause joy – and that is contagious.

I try not to sit around and fish for the words. It sucks to miss a beat, but it's better than missing the beat over and over.

I think there's ammonia in urine. A quick fact check would do me good.

Though the train station can get louder, you should hear the welfare office.

Add to it. Make some noise. Either that or it drowns you out – and who wants to drown?

This brings me to waves. Speaking of waves and drowning. Water waves. Sound waves. I guess light waves can drown out your vision. I wonder how that's different than blinding?

So you can obviously drown peoples' thoughts out with your own. This will cause them to get tired. Mentally fatigued. I'd been working on sending thought waves. Theta waves. Alpha waves. Gamma, Beta, whatever else. Low frequency energy. It washes people away. When pointed, it can do good. Or ill. It's an undeveloped science. Laughable by the people of the future. Eventually, thinking over each other will be as faux paus as speaking over each other.

DeShawn is the most famous person here because his mother keeps yelling his name.

Kick up your legs and relax, cause this is gonna be a while.

DeShawn must be bored. Maybe he's not used to meditating. Maybe he's pretending. Climbing on the desk, he was. Now that's entertainment. Now he's climbing on his mother. I think it's his mother. He could be a professional climber by the looks of it.

Sounds like it is his mother.

Sometimes you just need someone to touch you in the right way. Move you past the painful parts.

I never used to crack my joints, but lately it seems like a build up of fluid has arrived in my neck. Stiffness. Cartilage? Where fluid meets solid.

I guess I'm getting my wish. Growing another vertebrae. Growing pains. My neck is longer. It's more fun.

I don't like living life as if someone's going to come up and poke me. Fearing an interruption so much that I do nothing to interrupt. It's part of life, this interruption. I am not so great that I deserve it not. How to deal with it? Accept it. Fruit it. Give it energy when you can. You know if you should ignore it. Ignorance is essential at times. No doubt. It's like when words meet sound. Sometimes they have no meaning but the sound they make, and that is ignorance. Or is it ignorant to read too much in to things?

It is the opposite, Arrogant.

Ride the line between both, accepting them like railways. Railings on the stairway to truth. Hang on to them temporarily if you need to, but don't block the stairway.

I have a feeling releasing tension in one area causes it in another. And that it works the other way. Too much of either is no good.

Don't spend so much time worrying about the left that you forget about the right.

The upside to waiting in a giant waiting room full of people? You get some amazing smells.

Open, close. Close to open. I close my book to open it a moment later.

I'm not too focused on what happened before. I AM focused on a soft subjugation of my eminence. Though it's not really mine. Still, I lie.

Has someone ever told you they were lying? Did you believe them? Interesting that we have the power to do that as humans. There must be a reason for it.

Sometimes, I take the water from the urine in my bladder and absorb it. I've also done it with diarrhea. I'm sure it leaves behind some residue that would be better washed away. A salty, crystalline structure.

Don't let your eyes deceive you. They'll tell you what happened, but not what's about to.

Remember what's about to happen, because that's the way it works.

Let your deep self conscious tell your future.
Somewhere, you know what's coming. Where
knowledge meets reason. Or intelligence. Thought
meets provocation.

There's always some sort of reception, it's just not
always enough to spark (or vibrate) your
instrument.

It's nice that people get multiple chances. It's our
nature to learn from our mistakes. And it seems
that peoples' chances can get reset to chance
number one through good acts? I don't know,
exactly, but I've noticed it.

Everyone's a winner at the social services office.

I love people. The way they can be. It doesn't take
much, just enough.

Let love flourish. And this is coming from an atheist, agnostic.

The ology would be the study of "the?" I think. Don't quote me, even though I threw up a quote.

I've been much less noticed and much more respected since my hair was cut. It was probably the way I'd been wearing my hair which was in my face. Who wants to look at someone that can't see? No offense to the blind people, because you can see eventually. Ocular implants for anyone that needs them.

Also, if looking at the sun can cause blindness and also improve your vision, I bet if blind people were to regularly sun gaze they could see again.

The sunlight eats away the junk that clouds your vision.

Did I tell you I need to learn German to read Mein Kamf? I think having a goal will help me learn. It makes the learning a side effect of a tangible product.

Rather, a side advantage.

Kamf man. German 101.

You know what makes me feel good? Having a place to stay satisfies some of my feeling, but earning it satisfies the rest. Or at least, a large part of what I am.

On Facebook, people say Geute Nacht. I think that's how it's spelled. It's German, I'm learning.

I think it's legal to sleep in your car here. It's not in LA.

It's for your own protection, they say.

I admit, I exhausted the battery on my laptop getting wi-fi off of some network called dave. Drank some vegetable broth, ate some macaroni salad and some roasted pumpkin seeds. I'll roast them in my oven one day when I have one.

It got hot under my blanket last night so I cracked the windows. At least one mosquito made his way in here. Could have been a female. I think "women" are inherently human. You don't have women mosquitoes.

Anyway, that bitch showed itself one too many times. It went splat when I smashed it, and boy was it full of blood. I thought it looked red when I saw it earlier, though it could have been the light playing with me.

Ain't no free lunches. Hard work yields reward.
Especially smart hard work. That's one thing about
getting general relief from the state. It's awesome
but it's time consuming. They make it like a job.
No fucking around. Be here at this time for training
or you lose your benefits that you don't even have
yet.

This should be a book about the cosmos. If I were
in the woods, it probably would be, as I can see the
stars better. I'll blot out the names of the people in
this book. Replace them with something kitschy.

So my goal right now is to leave the state of New
York or get a job as a server, serving fine, delicious,
healthy food. Also stay with Mac in Astoria. His
dog is great.

I guess writing to write is fine. Like fine dining or a fine tipped pencil. Maybe I'm thinking of a felt tipped pen.

When I smoke marijuana I really get in to myself. Maybe I should warn people first. "I WILL GET IN TO MYSELF. DO NOT TAKE IT PERSONALLY. BE RELIEVED, I AM DOUSCHING IN FRONT OF YOU. ALL CAPS I WIPE MY MIND."

I just really feel the way I am. Some people get chatty. I do too. I push them. They push back. I stretch. I should just tell people - "I go in to full yoga mode when I smoke pot." Do not fear. If you need me, I'm still here for you. But you really have to need me and you really have to express it. It's been a crazy time in my life for seven years.

I wonder how long that will go on for. It's part excuse for bizarre behavior, part truth. Exposing the truth. I just don't want to get my teeth kicked in while doing a toe touch in public.

Loving to live. That is the positive way to say "not afraid to die?"

I love to live and live to love. I seek to benefit the human race and all other life forms on the planet and beyond. I will take care of my body. Animals that seek to make me food will be destroyed.

Now that's a funky one. "Make me food." If there is an animal that wants to make me food one night I hope not to destroy them. Like make me some food to eat.

But if there is some animal that wants to make food of me, like a mosquito, I will destroy it.

Is that love? Kill what would seek to eat you? Eradicate it?

Love is probably just some chemical rush and different levels/combinations at that. I'm going to put more apples in my diet, for love cometh from the stomach. And preservatives will stop it from reaching it's potential.

My camera's not good enough to capture it, but I can see the Freedom Tower lights out my window. Shooting straight up in to the sky. I guess life is supposed to be this beautiful. Grace of whatever.

People on bikes ride by. Cars fly by. It's after midnight, methinks, but the world churns. This living factory.

A bullet storm of high powered actuality. Kind of
like a nice drive. Maybe because I'm sitting in the
driver's seat, but instead of flying past everything,
everything's flying past me.

Oh radical television. To see what can be seen.
The words are like a can of worms and they can just
be ok. They can sound right. I don't want to be
muffled by redundancism, but I do want something,
to be heard.

When my focus becomes someone, I sit back and
relax and center again. It's the way it should be
right now. Narrative to pascism.

I used to watch cars rolling down the street, getting
ready to cross. I'd think "If I cross...right...NOW!"
And imagine myself bolting across the street.

We are faster than we are told, though there is nothing wrong with slowing down. Slow down to get there faster. Take it easy. Let those in front of you go ahead sometimes.

Sometimes, when you go too fast you get in to a wreck or get pulled over for fear of causing a wreck. In the car and psychologically.

Sometimes you just need to pull over in the highway of your mind and check for directions. Or deliver that text. The world's not perfect, and some things are time sensitive. The light from the Freedom Tower is pulling other light up with it. An odd optical illusion or infraction. It's happening and it's not – at the same time. So I talk about time.

Time

Time is motion. Time is a refraction of space. A bent logorythem of time. Logarithm. Could have been spelled a multitude of ways but this is no dictaphone.

I suppose that's why time goes faster and slower. It's a hyperactive result to it's base. Not only is it relative to its base, it can be any relation.

Anyway, thyme (hah) changes and shyfts depending on how you look at it. In a world where all "i's" are "y's" you may question your sanity. If all i's are y's and all y's are i's – well, what's the difference? - Convolution!

External time is relative to internal time. So it could be like watching a spinning hub cap on a wheel. It starts going so fast that it appears to be going backwards.

Like a spinning thought process. If it goes fast
enough, time may appear to slow down – or
compensate by going regular speed but then,
backward a way.

There is a thought time. Brain patterns are not
bound to our "time" the way a second hand on a
watch is. We are capable of thinking twice as fast
without realizing it. A watch is programmed not to.
Inversely, we can also think twice as slow.

There are many uses for this behavior. Changing
brain patterns can also change (or allow to change)
the patterns or things around you. Like a
quarterback and a receiver slowing down the
general clock time by speeding up their realization
patterns.

Sometimes, if you think a lot, quickly, panickly, the clock may have barely moved. Sometimes you can focus long stretches on something and see the clock time has passed greatly.

I've noticed, in meditation, 20 minutes will go by. Then when I look at the clock, only 2 minutes of that time have passed. Speeding up to slow down, or slowing down to speed up. It seems to age my soul but calm my body. Giving 20 minutes of rest in 2 minutes. It's a good tactic when I get up in the morning and have to be somewhere but am still tired.

It is connected to your gut. Good digestion makes good meditation. I like to lay with my arms over my head, flat on the ground, to raise my diaphragm.

123

I should tell you. I claim to be no expert on any of
the things I talk about in this book. I can only
speak from experience and make things up. I have
no intention of deception, but I will bend the truth
like a reed in the wind or a light in the stratosphere.
I come from another planet. Searching for life.
The problem is, everything on earth is carbon
based. Well, not everything. But a great deal of the
life. As a light based being, carbon seems moot. It
seems remote.

Anyone that comes to the Wellfare office and
expects to buzz through baffles me. It's a long ride.
Bring a book. Oxidize. Relax. Ride like a river.
On a river raft. The river isn't going to get you
there any faster if you complain.

Of course, you can paddle. But not at the wellfare office. Here, you sit. This ties in to speeding up and slowing down time. Maybe doing something like writing or thinking is like paddling on the mind river. Speed up or slow down your center to let things pass by and through you at a more accommodating rate.

I made the mistake of sleeping with my car windows cracked on the city streets. It was nice, the cool air, but the mosquitoes found their way in. I battled them for hours last night. Baited them in to my ear then swatted. That didn't work. I ended up finding success by letting them close then pulling away and flipping the light on. Their speed and agility is their weakness. They smear easily.

The dryness of the south must keep them away.

The end is the beginning. In an attempt to not be too wordy, I'll splay out what I think. I'm sure it means something to someone. I also think change (pen faded out)

I think what we can do is build a large enough community, communicating through the earth (maybe literally through the ground) so that if there is some ecological disaster we will be able to hold a society together despite violent factions that may break out.

Plastic printers printing guns

No one is white, no one is black. Not exclusively.

I get inspired to write a book.

Revolution with action. I was going to say revolution without action is just a thought process,

But thought process is action.

Direct connection with people is good. It's good.
It's bad.

I choose to sit alone and write, rather than interact
with a bunch of Occupiers because I find the
diatribe so exhausting. Am I destining myself for
lonely? Yes, if I ask the question. I sit in a street
park at 34th st & 6th ave. I like how they've
cordoned off areas of streets and now made them
sitting areas. I'm battling with the pencil. I don't
want to buy another pen because I have a bunch in
my car, so I'm going to carve this pencil with a
small knife from my bathroom grooming kit.

I went into my bag to find it and found dirty
earplugs.

Looks like I'll be sharpening this pencil with my fingernails. Always carry a knife. And a needle and thread & a lighter. As well as my first aid kit. Emergency surgeon.

The Frustration is palpable within the occupy movement. It's fledgeling. Race is still an issue, and so are semantics. The human race? K-9? White & Black? It drives me nuts. People like to identify, but that adherence to what we think we are will hold us back.

It smells like a mix of charcoal grill and sweet bubble gum and pollution. What a park. At least it's a nice place to write. I just snagged a table. The flat surface will take me higher and maybe someone will sit down with a pencil sharpener.

A man can dream. And he will. But at the same
time he will face reality, and sort of half ass it as
long as it works and shows no sign of stopping.

I used to watch kids in class get up and use the
pencil sharpener like it was a drug. Brag about
their pointy tips. I would just peel away the wood,
leaving a long, dull piece of graphite sticking out
the end of my pencil. Less likely to break, with the
amount of pressure I put.

The bell is ringing. Decision Time.

I'm definitely going to need a blade for this pencil.
It looks like a lion's mane. Which looks, oddly, like
a penis head stricken with genital warts. Thank you
health class.

I'm not even sure if Occupy is worth talking about, but it must be because I am. I came out almost a year ago – last October 2011. It was a mess. A rainy love fest that was over policed. There were racial issues deep within. People within the darker skin community upset that the lighter skin community had more press time. It sickened me. How do you even accurately talk about different races of people? Specific skin color? Shade? Ancestry? Either I've gotten past it partly or I want to. I don't understand mistrust. I will play the card but I don't like it.

I really believe that I need to stay apolitical about the whole thing and just play songs.

Like Bob Dylan. Outspokenly apolitical but writing about what was going on.
I don't want to judge but I will comment as blatantly as I will about what I see. Maybe it's influenced by my race, but I was raised to be good to people no matter who they are. Charles Manson deserves a chance. Laugh it off. He does.

Whether we're people, places or things, we're all nouns. And no one's better than a good book. Silly thing to say, maybe, but the art tends to outlive the artist.

I love pencils. The thickness is divine.

Alright, I sharpened my pencil on the corner of the license plate I carry around with me. It's extra, I only put one on my car. And since it's flat and metal it is desirable to have as a spine in my backpack. Support for the laptop. And papers. Less bending. More structure.

What's coming next? Probably a world of simplicity. Where grounding with the earth will give you a connective bond with all the other connectors. Bare foot. Like an internet. Not just talking about it. Talking about it sometimes, but doing it. I could probably do that at Fort Greene Park. Or any park. Feet to dirt. A great song. Put your feet to the earth and feel the tingling. Feel the energy sucked out of you where it hurts.

It keeps you warm and cold and it works with the wind. A real bonding. An earth bond. A slow degradation in to society. Maybe inevitably facing the same mistakes of the past; but let's document our travel so it's easier to overcome next time.

Ever had a tooth that's sensitive to cold? That's how it feels when the earth regulates your energy. I suppose it's alright because it is the earth.

I haven't turned my back on you, society. And if I've put my head in the sand, it's only to examine it. I'll tell you what I've found. I'll explain it in great detail.

It's food. I ate a leaf the other day. We can learn to eat grass.

It's not just the end, but a new beginning.

The wind blows my pages over to a clean slate. It tells me that it's a new day. Breathe that methane out and the oxygen in – deep in to your core to breathe the methane out again. This improves your sense of smell.

It's ok to smell the pavement. The trees, bushes, urine, perfume and doughnuts. It's sickeningly sweet. But, fuck it. Give it a smell. The ozone's ever present. That's O3. It's emanating off you. Soon, we'll be able to reconfigure the heat emanating off our bodies and use it to power machines. We already use it to power each other.

Horizontal or vertical they say at Occupy. They're forgetting about the Z axis. The third dimension. We don't just communicate side to side and up and down. We communicate around. Spherically. Taking all points in to account of this three dimensional palpatation.

I should elaborate reaching the end of my book even though it's not the end. I don't stop until the pages are gone. Maybe that's an obsession of mine.

I've never finished a book before. I'm not really sure how to. It's not really plotted, so how do I know if I've reached my destination?

I think this is the kind of book where I will open it to a random page and read a random passage. Or let the wind blow it to a spot and read that. I'll remember writing it. I'll remember sitting on that rock in Fort Greene park and talking to those kids, riding two bikes and a scooter. I did tell them I'd go back there.

This is probably just a piece of the puzzle. I'm not sure what shape, exactly. And it's not Tetris.

What I have found, though, is that the thoughts in your brain that seem so mundane are profound to some and deserve to be written down.

A Scorcese book. A sorcerer's poem. A book of lies and love and truth and poetry. Sometimes the stuff that rhymes doesn't rhyme at all. And the wind keeps blowing.

I've got a garden of books to write but this pencil is wearing down.

IanCrossland.Net

Made in the USA
Middletown, DE
31 May 2022

66470885R00086